THE
DECADENT
CONSCIOUSNESS

A
HIDDEN ARCHIVE OF LATE
VICTORIAN LITERATURE

FORTY-TWO RARE AND IMPORTANT TITLES
PUBLISHED IN THIRTY-SIX VOLUMES

EDITED BY

IAN FLETCHER &
JOHN STOKES

GARLAND PUBLISHING

THE HOUSES OF SIN

POEMS

Vincent O'Sullivan

Garland Publishing, Inc., New York & London

1977

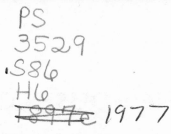

Bibliographical note:

The facsimile of *The Houses of Sin*
has been made from a copy in a
private collection.
The facsimile of *Poems* has been made
from a copy in the Yale University
Library (Iy.Os8.896p).

Library of Congress Cataloging in Publication Data

O'Sullivan, Vincent, 1872-1940.
    The houses of sin.

    (The Decadent consciousness)
    Reprint of the 1897 ed. of The houses of sin, pub-
lished by L. Smithers, London, and of the 1896 ed. of
Poems, published by E. Mathews, London.
    I. O'Sullivan, Vincent, 1872-1940. Poems. 1977.
II. Title. III. Series.
PS3529.S86H6 1977   811'.4   76-25930
ISBN 0-8240-2783-3

BY THE SAME AUTHOR

POEMS

A BOOK OF BARGAINS

THE HOUSES OF SIN

THE HOUSES OF SIN

BY

VINCENT O'SULLIVAN

LONDON
LEONARD SMITHERS
ROYAL ARCADE: OLD BOND STREET
1897

CHISWICK PRESS :—CHARLES WHITTINGHAM AND CO.
TOOKS COURT, CHANCERY LANE, LONDON.

CONTENTS

REMNANTS of passion, remnants of defeat,
Ye rags and motley of out-worn desire,
Unto my hearth-rug drag your torpid feet,
And light a barren fire.

Bleak days of idle sin with madness shod,
Wishes scarce wished before they had an end,
The fear of Satan, and the fear of God,
Now with the ashes blend.

Mean hours spent mourning worthless things of earth,
Sorrows and loves I was too tired to spurn—
Ye, and the weariness which gave ye birth,
Come hither now and burn.

THE HOUSES OF SIN

THE street lay tremulous in yellow light
    Which mingled with the blackness of the night ;
    Soft murmured laughter sounded everywhere,
And sobs like laughter glided on the air ;
While on the steps, grouped round each open door,
Sweet persons stood and gazed on Heaven's floor.
Then, as a perfumed wind came glancing by
And kissed me with its melancholy sigh,
And wooed me to its lair
Of flower-haunted rooms : " Would you go there ? "
A voice said low, and charmed my willing ear.
" Would you take part with those who give the cheer
In yon gay scene, and look on those who lie
'Neath every incense-freighted canopy ? "
Ah ! well I knew
That only to escape the horrid crew
Of daily tiresome deeds, the noisome crowd
Of those who seek themselves and seek aloud,
Who think austerity a prick of pin,
And folly call, to dignify it, sin,
I had all-hailed the Infamous !   Then " Yes,"
I said to him who soothed my loneliness,
And looked upon his face.

He was a man on whom some strange disgrace

Had settled in the morning of his years,
And bowed him to a life of shame and tears;
Pride and humility mingled in his mien—
The servant of the servant of a queen.
"Come, let us go!" he cried, and passed along
With hasty steps between the mighty throng:
Onward we pressed through crowds with laughter lit,
Till at a house where *Avarice* was writ
In scarlet letters, he said: "Get you in!
This is the first house in the street of Sin."
An ancient dame was sitting at a wheel
With which she spun the gold threads of her reel,
And all her threads she twined in little rolls
Around her bodkins, which were human souls.
"Here all is peace," quoth she; "but you descry
Just opposite a house of revelry:
There doth she dwell for whom I eat the dust—
My ever good and constant neighbour *Lust.*"
"Quick!" spoke my friend, "the revels now begin."
And lo! we sought the second house of Sin.

Throughout that night we passed from door to door
And saw all men on earth, as on the shore
Of various lands a traveller may see
Wreckage cast up by one great shuddering sea.
Now when the moon was highest, I descried
The state and splendour of the house of *Pride*,

And sought the gracious hostess, in whose eyes
A man looks once, then serves her till he dies.
And when the moon was waning, and the night
Was yielding to the day's encroaching light,
Haggard and bowed we dragged our way within
The portals of the final house of Sin.
Here two dark sisters did their arms entwine:
" My name *Anger*." " *Jealousy* is mine."
A banquet of strange dishes was outspread—
A banquet served by unforgotten dead
With wild entreating eyes
Which begged a respite from men's memories.

When I had tasted of a subtile dish
At this grave feast, behold! I had no wish
Left in my heart, but grew as one asleep
Amongst the dead, whose passions strong and deep
Are merged in longed-for, unexpected peace,
And give them ease.
So full of joy I cried out to my friend:
" Come, join this deathly feast and so make end!"
He wailed: " I dare not—dare not gather near!"
Then hung his head and wept: " My name is *Fear*."

MALARIA

AT sunset, when the shifting light
　　Fails in the marshes, what most fair
　　And sombre Spirit, robed in night,
　Comes floating down the waves of air?

Hot air that takes away control
　　From all my body's nerves, and falls
Like scented water through my soul.
　　Miasmas spread like perfumed palls.

A violet and yellow flush
　　Floats to intense skies like a spire:
It bathes my heart with secret hush
　　And fills my brain with dreaming fire.

Poison, dark goddess, is thy name!
　　Beside the rank and stagnant pool
Where thou dost live, there is no shame
　　In thy embrace: thy bed is cool.

Come, ere appears the steadfast line
　　Of outpost stars—ah! let thy breath
Kiss me, and press thy breast to mine,
　　Thou sweet grave harbinger of Death.

THE HOUR OF GHOSTS

WHEN the wind blows and stirs their earth-worn
faces,
Sometimes they wake and rise up from their
places,
Seeking each other's looks
In sad wise ;
Sad, sad they gaze at the buffeted elms,
And shew the vague dismay that overwhelms
(Scaring the crazy rooks)
Their tired eyes.

Wistfully then they strive to touch each other,
Yearning for life.   One murmurs: "Lo! my brother,
See you in yonder field
The red kine ?
They and that small white farm-house with the gable,
The garden, and the brown horse in the stable,
All that and all its yield—
All was mine !

"Now as I laboured on the brightling sward
I thought that life beneath the sun was hard,
That to lie here were peace,
Sleep, and death :

In yon square barn I took a rope one morn
And hanged myself amid the amber corn,
And swung till came full cease
To my breath.

"I had a red-haired woman for my wife;
A year past, when she saw me void of life,
Her weary strangling sobs
Bewildered me :
Now behind those lit windows she delights,
While I must lie here till the end of nights
Listing to the dull throbs
Of the sea."

Thus these old ghosts make converse in their woe,
While the day thickens and bats whir and go,
And in the twilight dream
Lad and lass :
Birds droop; the drowsy church-bell tolls for bed;
'Tis bed-time too for the forgotten dead,
Who in the light's last gleam
Sigh "Alas!"

THE VERGE

NOW midnight tolls, and up the stair
    Creep the wild visions of despair—
    Sin and Sorrow, Sin and Sorrow,
Creep to meet the trembling morrow:
Now midnight tolls from ancient clocks
Whose rusty strokes, like muffled knocks,
Fall on the heart, and frighten it,
Of one who mournfully doth sit
In a dark chamber dimly lit,
Surrounded by the violet breath
And glamour of approaching Death.

Like a white horse, which rushes past
The watcher and divides the blast,
On a bleak night on some wild shore
Where the strong breakers' massive roar
Drowns the resounding of its feet;
So terribly, so almost sweet,
Beside the dull and bitter sea
Of man's life passes silently
A sheeted ghost whose face is hid.
But never—never shall man rid
Himself from thinking of that face—
What its strange pallor, what its grace,
When the unveiling doth take place.

Can Heaven lie hid in grave-cold eyes?

Ah, at the midnight one man tries
To gather near, to lift the veil
And read upon that face its tale;
To gather near that dread and holy
Figure, and his melancholy
Shatter by a wild caress
In the all sombre silentness.

The face of her the lately dead,
New wandering from her little bed—
Shall it be as it once has been,
Or gray and horribly serene?
The eyes which he has closed, alas!
Have light, or stare like painted glass?
Her hair—oh! of her wilderness
Of hair, shall there be left one tress?

But lo, a hand has thrust aside
The veil—as when the moon doth ride
In Heaven she parts the blinding clouds
And scatters them in flying shrouds.
A filmy figure, almost air,
Bends slowly o'er the mourner's chair;
A sacred figure, grave and dim,
Seeks for his face and kisses him:

And at that kiss, from off the wall
The ghastly taunting shadows fall—
Writhe and expire there as they fall.
He dreams : a hush floats down the air—
Is this her mellow glorious hair ?
He dreams : then leaps from clutching years,
And sees her eyes are bright with tears.

DRUG

WHEN winds scream round the corners damp
        and chilly,
    And clouds of rain blot out the gas-lamp's flare,
While lean-faced, pale-eyed men take stand and glare
Upon the sin-soiled floor of Piccadilly,
And harlots of the pavement fling their silly
Maniac laughter in their great despair—
Sweet Drug! 'tis thou who draw'st me thence, to where
Sways languidly the dew-embroidered lily.

Light up the dusky caverns of my soul,
Light up the dead oppressive days, and shine,
Miraculous life-giver! where the scroll
Of hours is spent and charred: ah, come and twine
Thy soft arms round me! Now let tempests roll;
The pageant of thy spirit blends with mine.

THREE MOMENTS

I THE LOVER

THROUGH my garden to-night she will pass,
　　The lady who perfumes my dream,
　　And her feet through the dew-heavy grass
Will glide like a moon-silvered stream,
　　And the roses bend down
　　To catch scents from her gown,
Ere her soul lights my soul with its beam.

O Night, Queen of Love, kiss the stars!
　　Let nightingales lusciously sing!
Come fairies in gossamer cars,
　　And strange woodland moths on the wing:
　　　She will come, she will come,
　　　And the hours will be dumb
With the passion her purities bring.

II HUSBAND AND WIFE

　　Kiss my hair again, love,
　　　I forget
　　In your kiss the pain, love,
　　　And the debt.

21

Must this shameful sorrow
    Now begin?
Must I face to-morrow
    This red sin?

But indeed 'tis set so—
    Let it be!
Ah my eyes will wet so,
    Poor weak me.

Yes, I buy your life, dear,
    And your fame,
Even I your wife, dear,
    With my shame.

I had craved as treasure
    Any power
Which could give you pleasure
    For an hour.

Here it is at last, but
    Now 'tis come,
Past dreams are not past but
    Round me hum.

Still resolve is taken,
    I will swerve

No whit, nor be shaken :
  You I serve !

Here are all his letters :
  See, he's glad
Forging his own fetters—
  Foolish lad !

Madman ! to be dreaming
  I am true
Even in the seeming—
  Loved by you !

Fool ! to think snares thus planned
  Can entwine
Me who call *you* husband—
  You are mine !

Ha ! he's melancholy,
  For he missed
Touching lips all holy
  Since you kissed.

O my soul, my treasure,
  'Neath the sky
Two souls filled God's measure—
  You and I.

Whisper very low, love,
    Let your breath
Fan me—now I go, love—
    This is death.

III   THE LOVER

Earth's iron jaws are bound with scarfing snow,
Like to a man late dead whose mouth drops low.
(*Hush my Friend!   The tempest broods behind.*)

Long hours I watch a little scented glove,
And dream of noons I played and glanced with love.
(*Voices of dead children in the wind.*)

Sudden I found my playing was in vain :
I scratched between her breasts a crimson stain.
(*A scarlet light breaks on the purple sky.*)

She wronged me and she crushed me to despair—
That woman with the lustful raven hair !
(*A cold face snow-blanched by a veil doth cry.*)

I seized a poisoned knife and struck her dead :
To-night three coffins shall inclose her head.
(*Wolves in the winter have a hungry growl.*)

To-night the glory of her magic kiss
Shall stir the damp worms as they pry and hiss.
(*Wet leaves of cypress in the henbane bowl.*)

And my soul and the soul I loved so well
Shall mingle in the torment of God's hell.
(*Moan, wind! above the pit where lost souls howl.*)

LOVE IN TEARS

SHE saw me with my melancholy head
  Bent down among the grasses of the grave,
  Among the long grass as the blue wind sped,
Where I for my dead love did sadly crave,
And thought : Now does her mellow hair still wave
And laugh and glitter like the morning sea,
As when in old lost days it played with me?

She saw me with my face ground in the grass,
As through that place she went with hushed white feet,
And paused to touch my hair, and then did pass
Quickly unto the grayish lichened seat
And sat there moping : clouds were in her eyes,
As one who dreams a space or yet she dies.

O Love ! (I pondered in my aching heart)
Since you are dead—quite dead, and I have stayed,
Shall I not close my mind and take my part
In the queen's mouth of yon sweet idle maid?
Still jocund homesteads laugh, the months parade !
You never move, dear, nor the yearning pain.
We two looked long, then passed like ghosts in rain.

THE DANCER AT THE OPERA

I

THE dancer at the opera
    Had the calm eyes and mystic grace
    Of gray-clad holy nuns, but ah !
Her soul reflected not her face.

Her soul lay drunken with the vaunts
She tolled, like maddened bee, from lips
That gave her wondrous body chaunts—
White cloud which made her soul's eclipse.

And as one who drinks thirstily
Out of a cold and crystal well,
Is stricken at its depths to see
The slimy poisoned fungus dwell ;

So at rare times the youth who dies
Her sweets with slow kiss to explore,
Sees her soul weep behind her eyes,
Then pass and leave her as before.

II

One night the dancer was elate,
A night when stars made cold their beams,

A monarch was to hear in state
The best of Wagner's music dreams.

Before her mirror she prepared
(The thought just added to her bloom)
To win a triumph no one shared.
Her loveliness filled all the room.

The church-bells spoke the clock at six,
When throughout Paris at the tolls
Folk kneel before the crucifix,
And say " Hail Mary " for their souls

Wrapped in her furs she seeks the stairs,
And then descending gay of heart,
Humming light operatic airs—
Why does she pause and wildly start ?

Four men of grave and sombre mien,
Four men in funeral array
Bearing a coffin in between,
Are coming up and bar her way.

Imperiously her questions ring :
" What messenger for you has sped ?
For whom do you this coffin bring ?
Who in this house is lying dead ?

"Answer!"—One hastens to obey:
"We bring this coffin here for a
Mademoiselle who died to-day:
The dancer at the opera."

"Liars!" She springs from where she stands,
With face of ice and breast in flame,
To drag away the sable bands:
Upon the lid she reads her name.

She gains the street in blinding woe:
Think you she seeks the garish hall
Where the lights vie with gems?—ah no!
She kneels at a confessional.

III

Where the king sits the music sobs
With passion too acute for tears,
Then bursts forth in triumphant throbs
Till the stars tremble in their spheres.

He, listening to the mighty surge
Of sound, hears strangely mingling in
Some wild harp-notes: The devil's dirge
For sinners who have ceased to sin.

WOMAN OF THE MIST

TARRY yet a little while,
    Woman of the mist!
I am lonely in the rain,
Of your dream-hands I am fain,
    Pure cold amethyst!
Dear love, hear the thudding drums
Heralding the Death that comes
To entreat me with his smile:
Stay, oh stay this little while—
    Woman of the mist!

Will you leave me all alone,
    Woman of the mist?
One winged moment clothed in joy
Left me, as a child the toy
    That he erstwhile kist.
Ah! the night is thick and sore
And my soul weeps on its floor;
Whisper, dear, you have not flown—
Pity! I am all alone,
    Woman of the mist.

Your voice shall soothe my life no more,
    Woman of the mist;
You light the stars, and cannot know

How all the stabbing winds that blow
   Wound me as they list:
With empty eyes and vacancy
I watch the dull and crying sea,
And linger on the hard wild shore
For one who comes no more—no more—
   Spirit of the mist.

SHADOWS

THE passionate flowers with their wild surrender
Of colours and sweets they garbed at dawn,
The tumbling bees, and oh, the tender
Shadows of birds all over the lawn.

Often at night I see fair old places
Where linger the ghosts I would fain forget
Ah, they sleep a sleep, those white dead faces
Too sound for dreaming as I dream yet.

CHILDREN OF WRATH

L AST night I wandered in the Devil's close,
Crushed by the aching agony of those
Who know strange secrets which they must dis-
close.

I found him seated in a herbless plain
On two large stones, nor with him any train
Of courtiers, or throng of souls in pain.

Across the muffled sky wild lightning broke,
And ever through the air the acrid croak
Of ravens fell: then drawing near I spoke.

"Almighty Master, thou whose name is feared
Throughout the sick world, and whose heart is cheered
By suitors, why alone?" The Devil leered.

"Look round this land!" he cried; "let your eyes scan
Till they go blind this desert—in its span
You shall not find the footprint of a man."

I answered: "There is one. Behold! I kneel
To whisper shameful things, that I may feel
Thy dread praise for the horror I reveal."

Then Satan: "Rise! If you would serve me, keep
Your sins locked in your heart as herds fold sheep
At fall of night: sin silently and deep!

"Walk armoured as a saint in open day;
Blaspheme me, and the Sacred Office say:
My servitors to God the loudest pray.

"I love the virtue of the fools who lie
Besotted with celestial vanity—
Who think they cannot sin, and shall not die.

"To them I ever murmur: 'You do well;
The Holy Spirit in your soul doth dwell!'
For them I keep alight the fire of Hell."

I wailed: "O Master, thou whose name is feared
Throughout the sick world, and whose heart is cheered
By suitors, spare the people scorched and seared!"

FEAR AT NIGHT

BESIDE the crying river
　　Where night is cold and pale,
　　And gaunt trees groan and shiver
In the shrewd autumn gale,
I ever hear it wail.

It pauses when I pause,
Then moves distraught and wild ;
I follow it because
It cries like a sick child
Whose soul is good and mild.

Its hands explore the ground
All night while dark winds rave,
And heap a little mound.
It has a corpse to save :
It digs a shallow grave.

O God, let me awaken
If this Thing is a dream ;
Or let yon soul be shaken
Into the shadowy stream,
And hush its boding scream.

35

Or on this foul alarm
I'll steal with stealthy pace,
And hold it in my arm,
And feel its breath a space—
Then see it face to face!

OUR LADY OF THE FIELDS

WHEN night wraps in velvet fold
 All the gracious land and still,
 And the hour for sleep has tolled
In the village on the hill,
    Mary my mother,
Thou movest through the flocks of sheep
Where white tired lambs are fast asleep,
    Mary my mother.

The grasses touch thy dove-gray dress,
And thy feathery small feet press
The pretty daisies, which are sore
Thy pensive passing to adore;
While from thy silver rosary
Falls, dreamily and silently,
The holy dew upon the fields
To bless the pleasant harvest yields.

By the church where sleep the dead
Thou dost watch a strange blue bird,
Who beside each weary bed
Singeth low thy soothing word,
    Mary my mother;
Then from that place with eyes full mild
Thou leadest forth a good dead child,
    Mary my mother.

Blessed Virgin, see me too,
Ere thou lookest on thy Son;
Make me leap to thee anew!
Proud sins have my life undone
Forcing me thy grace to shun,
                   Mary my mother
Please cure me of the Old Man's spell,
Which leads me down the road to Hell
                   O Mary mother!

FRANCIS BORGIA AT GRENADA

IS this the Queen—this thing with fastened eyes
And face where foul corruption has its seat—
Is this the Queen? The erewhile gracious form,
Struck with a great paralysis, is left
A thrall to those who but a week ago
Kissed the poor earth she walked and deemed their
      lips
The purer for that sacramental touch!
And now she cannot seek her resting-place,
But to the piety of slaves 'tis left
To bear her corpse (her corpse!) within the church,
Where its strange grin and ghastliness affright
Majestic monuments and graven stones.
Her crownèd hair has dwindled into dross;
Her hand, which if a man kissed only once
He became sacred in the realm of Spain,
Has turned to that no lozel dog would lick;
Her cheeks, which striving roses sought to vie,
Are stiff and hard as clay becomes with cold.
She who swayed cities and the lives of men,
Governor of Arragon and Castile,
And ruler in the half-spheres of the world,
Rules not this box which I am set to guard.
Kind God, is this the Queen?
            Thought she of God?

39

I knew at Seville once an aged man
Who like a comely mantle wore his age:
His eye had light, his manner suavity,
The pressing years had fallen on him soft
As rain-drops fall on little children's graves.
Now, when he came to die, I was of those
Who knelt about his pallet watching him;
And as the vesper-bell from sun-red towers
Just floated through the dim and hushing air
He stirred, and "I believe in God!" he said,
And pressed the crucifix against his breast
And died.   Then being dead he lay at smile,
Like one who dreams a pleasant easy dream
And would be sorry if he were to wake.
　　　　Did she believe in God?
　　　　　　　　I seem to feel
That this enchaunting earthly potentate
(More horrid now than spectres from old tombs)
Did in the glare and circumstance of court,
The perfumed lie, the murmured compliment,
Forget that being ruler of this earth
She held her crown in fief to Heaven's King.
And lo! to-night her visage irks the space
And dusty firmament of wheeling worlds,
While through yon old man's grave-grass soft winds
　　　weep.
No monarch claims our loyalty but God.

We play our parts upon His outstretched hand,
And with our metaphysic subtileties
Make shift to prove our own magnificence,
And flaunt Him throning it among the stars.

To-morrow, haply, God will close His hand.

CALVARY HILL

To Stuart Merrill

WHEN Christ our Lord up Calvary Hill
　　Went stumbling on that dark Friday,
　　A crowd, with horrid taunts and shrill
Did follow all the grievous way :
Poor Simon followed with the rood,
And vain high-priests from west and south,
And pagan slaves, and traitor Jude,
　　And Saul of the gibing mouth.

Ah, well I wot that mild Mary,
When in a shed one starry night
She watched a crib with holy glee,
Had moaned and died then utterly,
Could she have seen this blinding sight !
Not one in all that screaming crowd
Took thought to pity His sore drouth :
He paused ; and then His bruised head bowed
　　To Saul of the gibing mouth.

As through the ruck a woman slips
To cleanse Christ's face with napery,
Knave Saul doth place his finger-tips
Within his mouth and pulls his lips

Apart, with visage foul to see !
Then as he blabbed and wagged his head,
And spat his curse with mien uncouth,
An angel came and struck him dead—
 Struck Saul of the gibing mouth.

Now, Blessed Lord, this bleak Yule night
When Thou dost look on small tired sheep,
Be good to us, keep from our sight
The elf-man and each evil wight
Who prowls about us while we sleep.
Keep us, dear God, from wily ruse
Of ghosts who bring the mists from south,
From spectres of the meanly Jews,
 And Saul of the gibing mouth.

HYMN IN MAY

I WHO have sung of Thee,
  Mother of Grace !
  On this night think of me—
    Give me a place,
    O Mother of Grace !
'Mid the souls that throng to Thy face.

For what I have done,
For what I have sung of Thee,
Mother, bring grace to me—
    Plead with Thy Son,
    That I may be one
With Him, my race run.

In this soft month of May,
Thou, little Queen Mary,
Dost pass in the prairie
    And rub Thy white feet
    In the rain-grass, which fleet
Springs Thine odour to greet.

And Thy skirts hang in view,
So that the poor souls,
Crowding round with their bowls,
May catch the light dew

Which falls from Thy hair
On the folk, here and there,
In the hot pleasant air.

And here let me be !
Of Thy hand I am fain,
That I may complain
Of my illness to Thee—
Of the illness which mocks,
Which gibes with town-clocks,
Till Death the gate locks.

Here, crying aloud,
With dolour and sweat
Let me cleanse me my debt,
That when in a cloud
Comes Thy Son, of souls bowed
I be one of the crowd.

AT THE GATE OF THE YEAR

PLUNGING through on a funeral gale
   The year sweeps out to die at sea,
   Under the mournful stars and pale
The gray thing hurries away from me.
Why do I stretch out anguished hands,
Why am I worn and dull with pain?
Sweet friend of friends, in the next year's bands
Will your face look on mine again?

The year sweeps o'er the wailing brood
Of breakers to his place of death;
While on the heights, where erst he stood,
The new year draws generic breath:
He flies, he flies through blinding sleet!
His form is wrapped in shrouding rain:
Heart of my heart, shall we two meet
And watch a year pass e'er again?

On the sea's margin breaks the light
And colour of the new year's dawn,
Thoughtful of spring-tide it takes flight
And lingers over wood and lawn.
Ah, weep not so! incline your head
Upon my breast, as you are fain:
Soul of my life, shall I be dead
Ere you will kiss mine eyes again?

46

THE FULL MOON

ABITING wind and harsh
Doth wail a sobbing tune,
And now glooms o'er the marsh,
A wet and angry moon.

She shines upon the waste
Low-seated in the sky ;
I cross myself in haste
For fear of her red eye.

On moor-lands and on streams
She rolls an eye blood-red,
And in her sluggish beams
Dance the unhappy dead.

Then from the buried sands,
Through sad waves chaunting low,
The drowned stretch up their hands
And toss them to and fro.

O moon, the lost souls keep
Their Sabbath 'neath thy stare,
And my lost soul doth weep
In passionless despair.

A SILKEN LADDER

I

THE lights within the little distant town
   Come out like evening plants at eventide,
   And struggle with the dusk, as from the side
Of starry Heaven God lets the darkness down ;
The moist breath of the sweet drenched earth is blown
Across my face, and oh, to-night I ride
Upon that breath, and watch, when day has died,
The darkness add a glory to your crown.

O Love, these first steps in the drowsy lane,
These magic moments—whither do they tend ?
To-morrow shall the morn be gray with rain,
Or sunlight with the fragrant pathway blend ?
You leave me half in gladness, half in pain,
Like weary pilgrims at their journey's end.

II

I sometimes have this fancy in the rain :
I think the soothing rain those poignant tears
Wept silently beside the troubled biers
Of strange dead hopes, which, flying in their pain

Skyward, drop gloomily to earth again,
And, like forgotten words of flouted seers,
Bring back the buried terror of old fears,
And rust a cherished treasure with their stain.

Still, when on dreary days I see you part
From sheltering house, and leave the dainty trace
Of your thin foot in muddy lanes, and dart
Laughing through showers with mountain-maiden's grace,
I, looking from the prison of my heart,
Rejoice to know my tears shall kiss your face.

III

Methought I was a prisoner lying dead
In a close room of some grave citadel,
Where no white gleam did penetrate to tell
Of day outside and sunny hours that sped ;
But horrid dark was there, and round my head
Strange vermin crawled : when sudden in the cell
A warm light broke ; the damp walls shook and fell ;
Around my feet the hushed grass carpet spread.

My fantasy was mated in this wise :
Sullen I paced the noisome yelping street
Hating its breath, when for a dear surprise
You, wrapped in gracious musing, I did meet !

D

I met you and looked deeply in your eyes,
And lo ! I felt the town was strangely sweet.

IV

Like the assaulting sea with fury shod
Hurling gray breakers on an iron coast,
Or like the passionate music of the host
Of large-eyed youths who stand on Heaven's sod
Chaunting before the bannered towers of God—
To these I liken the strange power of lost
Delicious memories, and stronger boast
Than these the strength of love's all-touching rod.

A wondrous night still holds me with its spell !
Alone you walked the garden, the hot air
Hung heavily : enchaunted by the smell
Of witching flowers, you dipped your fair
And star-bathed bosom in their dewy well,
While the fond lilies kissed your gloomy hair.

V

As youthful playmates gambolling in joy
Spring suddenly from rapture to dull hate,
And glaring madly snap the bond of fate,
Not knowing man is fashioned by the boy,

And toss their passion like a broken toy,
(Each striving fierce with his afflicted mate,)
Bite hard and gibe, until they find too late
That stings which come in hours, for years annoy:

So all the holidays we once thought sweet,
And all the festivals we once held dear,
Are mowed by grief as fields the reapers mow;
And when I hail your shadow glinting fleet,
We touch hands for a breath in icy fear—
Two passing phantoms trembling in the snow.

OUT OF THE CLOUD

THAT fiend who tricked out like a saint
    Did haunt a most unhappy youth,
    And wall it in, and coarsely taint
Its whiteness with the lees of truth,

And choose for instruments the fools
    Who prate of duty to themselves,
Who fish for virtue in cess-pools,
    And line with lies their mental shelves,—

He is not dead, though Youth is dead,
    And Age, Youth's weary son, has smashed
The walls which held his sire and fled!—
    He hunts the thing he erewhile lashed.

A scowling ghost with scorching breath
    He follows hard, and shall not cease
Till God speaks through the mouth of Death
    And smites the sombre silences.

VALE

A SWORD has come between us: let us part
While yet our eyes in some vague way entreat
Each other; and a something near the heart
    Makes me linger at your feet.

Oh, what to me the Love whom men call Lord!
The maddened moments which ere long estrange;
The fashioned smile; the evil poisoned word;
    The subtile dexterous change?

Yea! though our listeners are but the flowers,
And soft winds be the bonds which us enchain,
And sweet the passing of the shining hours,
    Comes soon the ultimate pain.

The soft impassioned summer-time is over,
The fragrance of its coloured dreams is past;
Here in its place is winter's blanching cover—
    Here comely peace at last.

THE LONELY WOMEN

THE lonely women wist not of the hours
　　Which make the burthen of their dim despair,
　　Nor know they if the years bring sweets or sours :
As Sorrow's path grows broader in their hair
The lonely women wist not of the hours.

The lonely women twist and twine a wreath
Of blood-stained flowers which decked them in their
　　　　youth,
And see not Terror with his gleaming teeth,
And never see the pearl-eyed face of Truth.
The lonely women twist and twine a wreath.

Around them move the phantoms of the dead
Who close their ears to words, and in the street
'Tis not the crowd they gaze at, but the head
Of one to whom their lips were erstwhile sweet :
Around them move the phantoms of the dead.

And bitter pleasures which they never share
Press tepid kisses odourous of the tomb ;
For on their gray, cold feast-days they prepare
A welcome for the ghosts that throng the gloom,
And bitter pleasures which they never share.

No wine-soaked sponge your constant torture lulls
Ye martyrs ! as through life you bear your cross,
And reel beneath it to a place of skulls ;
And there, when on a grievous bed you toss,
No wine-soaked sponge your constant torture lulls.

O lonely women, I have looked on you
And seen the pain of your unheeded sighs,
And marked the grief you struggled to subdue ;
Yea, when forgotten tears were in your eyes
O lonely women, I have looked on you !

A SLAVE OF THE STREET

STANDING at draughty corners she will mutter
   Hoarse snatches of old songs with vague regret ;
   And then, remembering the erstwhile coquette,
With mincing walk and sodden smile and flutter
Hasten to greet the sweetheart, who with stutter
And heavy drunken feet is left her yet :
Till she, becoming drunk too in his debt,
Feels the earth rise and tumbles in the gutter.

Waked roughly from sweet dreams of country lawn,
She gathers up her coil of muddy hair,
Adjusts it gingerly, and tries to fawn
On cabmen to accept her charms for fare :
But when the saving lamps go blind at dawn,
She laughs her curses in the vacant air.

TO AN ENEMY: WHEN DYING

YES; you have won ! and so you linger there
　　While the lights wander from my windowed eyes,
　　And words I would have spoken, trail off sighs,
That you may gloat upon my last despair,
And hear me shout when to the soul God cries—
The soul, which but for you, He had found fair.

Are you content ?—Then hearken to my curse:
For every good you taught my soul to shun,
May your hard fingers rot off one by one,
And all diseased, in you, find something worse;
Yea ! as you smile, and turn my corpse to fun,
May your lips shrivel when you pass my hearse.

Ah peace !　The words I stammered are unsaid:
Your fleering laugh is token that I rave:
The hungry worms are crawling from the grave,
And you are stooping low across my bed:
But O mine enemy ! a boon I crave :—
Fold down your eyes ere you behold me dead.

A PRAYER

THE God who sends the stricken
Winds, fever-fed, to quicken
The glooms that round them thicken
Who pray to Him at night,
On Judgment Day shall sunder
His toys, and crush them under,
And stab them with His thunder,
And with His lightning smite.

From morning till the even,
By seven and by seven,
The stars shall fall from Heaven
To scourge the groaning earth ;
And winter pinch in May-time,
And weeping fill love's play-time,
And ghosts appear in day-time
To strike the lips of mirth.

The God who stamps and places
Sin's wounds on aching faces,
And with His finger traces
The lines of tears and sweat,
Heeds not the wretches crying :
" A Hell here full of sighing,
And Hell, O God, at dying—
Is this a righteous debt ?

58

"Strike down with Thy great sabre
My kindred and my neighbour,
The mothers in their labour,
   The children in the womb ;
Ah, drive us from our sadness
To welcome lust with gladness—
To rapine and to madness,
   So we forget our doom."

THE RIVALS

WHEN Death drawn near felt warm the breath
of Life
Her arms withdrew; for she was weakened
sore:
And "You can be my lover-friend no more;"
(She said to him hot panting through his strife)
"I should have held you closer than a wife,
And pressed you warmer to my bosom's core,
But Life's gray dogs came barking at you rife,
And held poor you and all the grace you wore."
"But Death" (he cried), "my fair and dreaming girl,
I did not mean to live when you came calling;—
'Tis thus by chance one oft the great love misses!
Ah! draw to me, and soft my life-wings furl,
For even now the hands of Life are falling,
And I am yearning for your cold white kisses!"

THE VOICE OF THE WINDS

WARM wind, whispering high and low,
    Tell me which way did my lost love go.
      (Hear the south wind sighing far out to sea !)
"Oh, I passed o'er a land where soft voices say
A sad 'Dona Pacem' for dead folk alway :
'Mid a countless host thy lost love was there,
With pure white stars in her shining hair ;
    And she smiled at me,
    As one who is free
From grief and strife and all misery."
(So the south wind sighed from the sounding sea.)

Warm wind, whispering high and low,
Tell me which way did my lost love go.
(Hear the west wind wailing far out to sea !)
"I come from the court of a glorious king,
Where a choir of maidens doth sweetly sing :
Amongst the brightest she brightest shone,
But eyes were sad, and she seemed alone :
    Then she looked at me
    And she bent her knee,
And I heard her prayer and it was for thee."
(So the west wind wailed from the restless sea.)

Wild wind wandering to and fro,
Tell me which way did my lost love go.

(Hear the east wind shrieking far out to sea!)
" I come from a region deserted and drear,
Where spectres shudder in frenzied fear :
'Mid those phantom forms thy love in the frost
Wrung her hands and wept like a soul that is lost,
    While she cried to me,
     'O wind, that we
Might be as free as the wind is free !'"
(So the east wind shrieked from the cruel sea.)

Wild wind, wandering to and fro,
Shew me how I to my love can go.
(Ho, the north wind howleth far out to sea!)
" In cheerless churchyard by crumbling tomb—
Dank and heavy and fraught with gloom—
She stands, and knows that when life is sped,
With its flame and fever, all hope is dead.
    'Hope not for me—
    I shall never be free,'
Is the message she charged me to bring to thee."
(So the north wind howled from the sobbing sea.)

62

GOD'S HOUR

IN the hot fading light
    I see, I see,
  The Spirit of God
Move down over me ;—
An odour of flowers in His wings,
And sweetly He sings—He sings
  To me, to me,—a poor clod.

In flaming battle rack,
  And give and smite,
I look in God's eyes,
  And the eyes are full bright
With light, leaping fire,
While He says : " My desire ! "

And grasps by the hand
  Me, halting and failing,—
  A wild sinner haling
Up to His white Throne ;
While the scent of His hands
Works off my drear bands,
  And old sins go wailing.

He leans from His throne,
  And His lips touched with lilies

Murmur: "Listen! My will is
That you be Mine own:
    And the soft gray-eyed moon
    Shall kiss you white soon."

And the angels with faces
    Tinged red from the sun,
    Bow down, one by one;
For a sinner craves graces:
    Well they know that our power
    Is God's breath in God's hour.

FOR THE END

AS sweetly comes to those this world calls mad
  The thought of calm worlds without scream or
      cry,
So is it unto man when he is sad
Pleasant to think that he shall surely die.

The sick and throbbing child upon its bed
Murmurs of streams, and for the sea doth rave ;
So, on this fevered earth, my thoughts are led
To dwell upon the coolness of the grave.

CHISWICK PRESS :—CHARLES WHITTINGHAM AND CO.
TOOKS COURT, CHANCERY LANE, LONDON.